UMM AYA

Musa and his First Fast

Learn about Ramadan with Musa, Bilal and Aya

First published by MH Publishing 2021

Copyright © 2021 by Umm Aya

All rights reserved. No part of this publication may be reproduced, stored or transmitted in any form or by any means, electronic, mechanical, photocopying, recording, scanning, or otherwise without written permission from the publisher. It is illegal to copy this book, post it to a website, or distribute it by any other means without permission.

This novel is entirely a work of fiction. The names, characters and incidents portrayed in it are the work of the author's imagination. Any resemblance to actual persons, living or dead, events or localities is entirely coincidental.

Second edition

This book was professionally typeset on Reedsy. Find out more at reedsy.com

Contents

Foreword to the Second Edition	iv
1 Musa learns about fasting	1
2 Musa tries to fast	5
3 Musa shares his story	9
4 Tarawih Prayers	12
5 Musa's mini-fast	15
6 Ramadhan evening relaxation time	18
7 Breakfast Cookies	21
8 Story time	24

Foreword to the Second Edition

This is the second edition of the book entitled *'Musa and his First Fast'*. I have updated the title from the previous one, as well as having updated the questions that are present at the end of each chapter. I wanted to ensure that the questions reflect a multi-faith audience and to ensure that other faiths are captured within the questioning and the thinking around the subjects. The reason for this is that whilst many people will come to this story with a keen desire to understand about the way in which Muslims experience the month of Ramadhan and the concept of fasting, I also wanted to highlight that Islam is not the only world faith that has a tradition of fasting within it, and to highlight the similarities of faith, rather than the differences. The illustrations have not been updated, and are still very entertaining and enjoyable for children!

With much love,

Umm Aya

1

Musa learns about fasting

One Sunday morning, Musa was playing with his toys when his Mum called him for lunch. He could smell cheese, its aroma rising up the stairs, and he was excited about eating cheese sandwiches. He went to the bathroom to wash his hands, as it was the *sunnah*.

He ran down the stairs, and when he entered the kitchen, his little brother and sister, Bilal and Aya, were already at the table enjoying their lunch. Musa sat down and he read his '*bismillah*'.

As they all sat eating, Bilal and Aya giggled away and made funny faces at each other. Musa made a really funny face, and they both burst out laughing. Musa knew that his mother loved cheese and thought that she would be having a sandwich too. But he was surprised to see that his mummy and daddy were not eating anything. He wondered why, and thought it might be something to do with Ramadhan, which his parents talked about a lot.

Musa notices his Mummy and Daddy haven't eaten or drunk anything all day

As Musa was a very brave boy, he asked his mummy about what he had noticed, "Mummy, why haven't you eaten your cheese sandwich yet?"

She lovingly cuddled him and said, "Son, Ramadan is a holy month during which we fast from sunrise to sunset."

"You can't eat or drink during the entire day?" Asked Musa.

"Yes, my dear boy, but there is a wisdom behind that. Fasting teaches us many qualities such as self-discipline, self-control and also sacrifice. God had told people to fast even before the Prophet Muhammad. Allah has told us about this in the Qur'an, that he had told the Jews and Christians to fast so that we can be more mindful[1]" said his mummy.

" Also, by not eating and drinking, we feel the suffering of those who are less fortunate" explained his Father.

Musa's parents explaining the meaning of fasting to Musa

---

[1] *"You who believe, fasting is prescribed for you, as it was prescribed for those before you, so that you be mindful of God"* (2:183)

***

Questions

1. Can you xplain what is happening in the pictures?
2. What does the word '*sunnah*' mean to you?
3. What does the word '*mindful*' mean to you?
4. Can you draw what it must be like to fast whilst living in a desert?
5. What does the '*bismillah*' mean? What is its full meaning in English?
6. Describe what sunrise and sunset means?
7. How long is a fast in Ramadhan where you live? (in hours)

[Research topics if interested/relevant to the child's age/ability]

1. Which other faith communities fast around the world?
2. Where in the Qur'an has Allah said that he had also told Jews and Christians to fast?
3. Could you have 2 conversations with your friends at school about fasting, and discuss what it means to you, and also ask if they have any questions about it.

2

Musa tries to fast

Later than night, Musa kept thinking about fasting and imagining himself in the desert without food or drink. That's when it occurred to him; the following day, he was going to try to not eat or drink until sunset. Neither Mum nor Dad knew about Musa's plan.

The next day was the first day of the summer holidays, and it was also the first time Musa had tried to to fast. He played with his siblings to pass time and he had lots of fun playing catch with them. It was nearly noon, and he was getting a bit hungry now.

Meanwhile, his mum has just finished preparing oat cookies. Musa loves oat cookies! They are his favourite snack. The smell was exquisite. Once the table was set, the children assembled around the table to eat the delicious cookies. Mummy said, "Ok children, remember to say your *bismillah*, and then eat your lovely yummy cookies." She then left the kitchen. Musa tried to resist the urge to eat...

Musa resists the oat cookies

However, by now he was too hungry, and felt like he couldn't wait anymore. Slowly, he walked over, and picked up two cookies. After briefly hesitating, he gobbled up both oat cookies at once!

Musa eating two oat cookies at the same time!

'Oh no what have I done', thought Musa.

"'I know what"', he said to himself, "I must tell Mummy, what happened". And with that, he started looking for his mummy all over the house.

* * *

Questions

1. Can you explain what is happening in the pictures?
2. What does the word '*exquisite*' mean?
3. What is your favourite food/snack/drink?
4. Why did Musa want to tell his mummy what happened?

3

Musa shares his story

Musa found his mummy working on the laptop, and he ran to her and cuddled her.

"What's the matter my dear child?" asked Mummy.

"After you told me about how Allah wants us to fast, I wanted to do it too. Today I was fasting, but the oat cookies you made for us are so delicious that I just couldn't resist them!" explained Musa.

"Oh my dear son, don't worry at all. In fact, you're only a child at the moment and you don't have to fast yet. But I am sure Allah will reward you for your effort!" said Mummy.

"What? Even though I failed?" asked Musa.

"When you try something and you don't succeed, Allah still loves that effort, as he wants us to try" replied Mummy.

With that, Musa give his mummy a tight squeeze and went to find Bilal, Aya and Danyaal.

Later that day, when Daddy had also finished his

work for the day, Musa told his family about what happened. They all laughed together with Musa, as they all knew how much he loved delicious oat cookies!

Musa sharing his story with his family.

Daddy also smiled and said, "My sweet boy, you remind me of myself. When I was your age, I ended up eating on my first try. Don't worry, soon you'll get used to it."

"How about tomorrow morning you try a mini-fast, starting after breakfast and finishing at lunch?" suggested his Mother.

"Thank you Mummy for encouraging me, I will do my best." replied Musa.

* * *

Questions

1. Why did Musa's mummy tell him not to worry?
2. What did Musa's mummy mean when she said 'you're only a child and you don't have to fast yet'?
3. What other types of people do you think do not have to fast?

4

Tarawih Prayers

The parents went to the kitchen to prepare the '*iftar*'; a feast everyone look forward to after the day's long fast during the month of Ramadhan.

When *iftar* time arrived, all the children of the family gathered around the table. The parents said they had an announcement to make.

"After we finish eating tonight, we will pray the *Tarawih* prayers with the family on Zoom" said their Mummy.

"What's *Tarawih* Mummy?" enquired Musa.

"*Tarawih* prayers are night prayers my dear child. They take place after Isha', and we can ask for anything from God". Answered Mummy as she looked very excited.

"Are we doing it on Zoom because of the germ problems?" wondered Danyaal.

"That is right, because of the coronavirus problem and the new rules to help all of us be safe, we can't go out and pray together", said Musa's Father.

Once the family heard the call of Isha' prayer via Mummy's phone, they all gathered in the living room while Musa's father placed the laptop on the table and called the family on Zoom.

Daddy being the Imam of Isha' prayers at home

Daddy was the leader of the prayers, who is also called the Imam in Arabic. Bilal, Musa and Danyaal stood together, and Mummy and Aya stood together. Daddy then started the prayer with '*Allahu Akbar*' which means God is great.

* * *

Questions

1. What is *Iftar* time locally where you live?
2. What is the name of the night prayer?
3. What does the word '*Imam*' mean?
4. Why do we sometimes use words from the Arabic language?

5

Musa's mini-fast

The following day, Musa woke up with a new spirit and the excitement he felt was incomparable.

At breakfast time, Mummy prepared a lovely *suhur* meal, which is what is eaten before the fast begins. Mummy gave Musa dates and yogurt, along with some orange juice and an egg sandwich.

After *suhur*, Musa did some drawing and was playing with his favourite dinosaurs. When Bilal had his snack time, Musa just walked past and resisted the urge to have a biscuit and Bilal was very surprised.

Musa was then busy playing with Bilal and Aya until he heard the call of Zohr prayer.

Musa's mother called him for lunch and expressed how proud she felt by her son's commitment. He could not be happier.

Musa resisting oat cookies once more. Successfully!

He prayed Zohr prayer with his family, then went to join his little brother and sister who congratulated him for his accomplishment. They all jumped on the bed celebrating Musa's achievement. The joy the little children felt was extraordinary.

Musa is very happy about completing his first mini-fast!

* * *

Questions

1. What are the names of the 5 main prayers in Islam?
2. What is s*uhur*?
3. What would you like to eat for s*uhur*?

6

Ramadhan evening relaxation time

That evening, the family gathered to watch Minions; a film on Netflix about Musa's favourite film characters. Musa's mummy also prepared mint tea, juice and homemade oat cookies. He was so happy to be with his parents and siblings, whom he considers as his best friends. Musa loves watching TV together with his family, and it is one of his favourite things to do.

RAMADHAN EVENING RELAXATION TIME

The family watching TV together

Everyone enjoyed the show and Musa enjoyed the cookies too. He loves his mummy's oat cookie recipe.

"Mummy, these cookies are so delicious!" said Musa.

"I know my dear boy, they're your favourite" she replied.

"How about tomorrow morning we make some for breakfast?" asked his Father.

"Really Dad?" exclaimed Musa, jumping for joy.

"Yes son, your mummy and I will make them for you." replied his father.

"Me and Bilal, Aya and Danyaal can help you." said Musa.

"Of course, you can my dear children, but now it's time for your bedtime" said Musa's Mother.

* * *

Questions

1. What's your favourite TV programme?
2. What's your favourite snack to eat?
3. Who are your best friends?

7

Breakfast Cookies

The melody of the birds chirping announced the beginning of a new day. Musa woke up in an excellent mood. He woke his siblings, then they all rushed downstairs to go help their parents in the kitchen. The parents were delighted and gave their children a simple task to do.

"Your Daddy and I will put the ingredients in a bowl, and each one of you will stir the mixture in turn using a whisk." said Musa's mummy.

Mummy and Daddy making oat cookies for the children

Once the kids had finished stirring, the parents poured the mixture into the cookie mould and then put it into the oven.

Whilst Musa and his siblings were waiting, they played a game of guess the vegetable. Each one had to close their eyes and guess the vegetable from the shape of it. They all loved this game, and Aya was very good at it indeed!

When the cookies had finished baking, Musa and his siblings were eagerly waiting for their parents to serve them breakfast. The whole family then sat and enjoyed the homemade cookies.

* * *

Questions

1. Do you have any siblings?
2. What games do you like playing?
3. Do you help your parents in cooking and baking?

8

Story time

For the rest of that day Musa played with his siblings outside in the garden. They all love to play football. After a full day of playing outside, Musa was very tired and fatigued. It was about 8 o'clock. Musa brushed his teeth, got into his pyjamas and settled comfortably in his bed. He waited patiently for his mummy to come and read him a bedtime story.

That day, the book Mummy was reading to Musa was about Islam and its connection with the holy month of Ramadan. While reading the book, Musa's mother explained to him that the verses of the noble Qur'an indicates that it descended on the faithful Prophet on a blessed night in the month of Ramadan[2]. The night is called Laylat Al-Qadr; it is in the last ten nights of Ramadan and the name means the night of power. In the book, it also talked about how Muslims practice

---

[2] Surah 97: Al-Qadr

i'tikaaf in the last ten days of Ramadhan. *I'tikaaf* is practising being quiet and alone so that we can focus on Allah *ta'ala* and learn more about Islam.

Musa sleeping in his bedroom

A few moments later, Musa seemed sleepy and started yawning. His Mummy turned off the lights and left the door open. The beauty of the moonlight illuminated the bed in which Musa slept peacefully.

***

Questions

1. What sports do you like playing?
2. What is *Laylat Al-Qadr*?
3. What does *Laylat Al-Qadr* mean?
4. What is *I'tikaaf*?

www.ingramcontent.com/pod-product-compliance
Lightning Source LLC
Chambersburg PA
CBHW040418100526
44588CB00022B/2870